summer honey winter rain //

sarah schwab

for my Busia.
for embracing every season

© 2018 Sarah Schwab

All rights reserved. No part of this book may be used or reproduced in any form without written permission from the author except in the case of brief quotations.

Self-published in the USA with international distribution.

ISBN-13: 978-1718601352
ISBN-10: 1718601352

Contact the author: sarahschwabpoetry@gmail.com
@_sarahschwab #summerhoneywinterrain

autumn..........................11-33

winter........................... 35-59

spring..............….........63-87

summer…....................89-115

*this little book is for the days you feel empty.
for the days you miss your grandmother.
for the days you want to hold your heart
outside of your body.
for the days you ache with tenderness.
or joy. or love. or loss.*

this book is for you. and for your friend who reminds you to love yourself. and for your mother who taught you how.

I hope it feels at home in your hands. I hope coffee stains mark up the cover and folded edges consume the pages. I hope something in here fills you up and pours you empty. I hope you are reminded of your power. and your vulnerability. and all the ways your heart sings to you. and all the ways you dance along.

//autumn

summer honey // winter rain

strip your leaves and let your cells turn red.
watch everything around you give into itself.
notice the softness of the sky.
find the freedom in letting go.

- we wait all year to remove the parts of ourselves
  we no longer need

I cannot get enough of you.
you
who drips honey from my lips
who sings inside of my bones while I'm sleeping
you
who tastes like autumn air and warms my throat with
each sip
you
who
cracks open the soles of my feet
and
fills me up
with every tender thing I forgot how to hold.

I cannot get enough of you.

you poured your soul into my hands

>it was the
softest
heaviest
loudest
thing
I've ever held

pay attention to the part of you
that falls in love first

words form around my mouth like
new beginnings.
familiar sayings with new intentions.
feelings that don't match the outside
but feel at home in the spaces between my
ribcage.
I am living here now.
it is frightening and it feels of fire.
but I will let it happen.
I will watch as it forms around the curve of my spine
inside of my palms
between each eyelash.
I will feed it when it asks to be fed.
I will let it flower inside my bones.
I will let it wrap my soul in newness.
I will let it be.

- don't forget to feed the beast // when beasts become

I am making a new home with you.
a home with
old books on every counter
and hazy kisses before bed.
half-filled glasses of whiskey on the kitchen table
and a drawer full of spices ready for tomorrow's dinner.
with writers block
and dancing in the mirror.
old stories pinned to walls, coffee stains on all the covers.
candles burning while we sleep
and guitar strings being tuned.
journals of yesterday's secrets that we've shared
a million times over,
not afraid to say it aloud anymore
because
our conversations taste like honey
and feel just as sweet.

I could live forever in this world.
I could live forever with you.

- awake

you feel like the moon
the way you move tides within me

I am in love.
I picture your sleeping face
as I close my eyes at night,
knowing that when I wake up at 3 in the morning
searching for something familiar,
my arms will wrap around your torso
and I will take a deep breath into the nape of your neck
and I will be okay.
I hear your I love you's
echoing
throughout every space in my ribcage,
generating warmth
filling me with a kind of comfort
that I only used to feel on full moons.

- equinox

sarah schwab

                    I still do not know what to do with hearts
                                      besides eat them

                    I took apart my whole body
                                piece by piece
            grabbed each of your hands and made you hold
                                  all of me

                    you didn't know what to do with it
                    my torso slipped through your fingers
                    my spine tumbled over your palm
                        parts of me landed on floor
        collecting around your ankles like forgotten trophies
                    for competitions you never entered
                         a prize you never wanted

                            I can't blame you for
                                  rejecting
                                  something
                            you never asked for.

-   (stop giving yourself away)

lay me naked beneath my faults.
I will give you 100 more.
it's a gift we have.

women.

we practice removing our skin each morning before a
mirror. replacing it with someone new.

do not call me soft.
I am made of fire and scars and sharp edges.
I am thorns and cracked sidewalks.
I am the burn on your tongue
and the sting in your eyes.
I am too bright
too full
too loud
too be anything you can fit in your palm
without burning through to the other side.

- womyn

dress in short skirts and tight pants. show every inch of your holy body. they will make you feel bad for calling it holy. they will tell you you're worthless. they will wrap their own figures in all of the fabric you left behind and then try to smother you in it. take off another layer. feel the sunlight bounce off your naked flesh. your skin can part seas. can save lives. can wade on water. you were reborn into this body. show as much of it as you want.

- things they don't teach you in catholic school pt. 1

                                they rip holes in us
                           and wonder why we're sinking

- waterlogged

femininity is not weakness.
femininity is not weakness.
femininity is not weakness.
femininity is not weakness.
femininity is not weakness.
femininity is not weakness.
femininity is not weakness.
femininity is not weakness.
femininity is not weakness.
femininity is not weakness.
femininity is not weakness.
femininity is not weakness.
femininity is not weakness.
femininity is not weakness.
femininity is not weakness.
femininity is not weakness.
femininity is not weakness.
femininity is not weakness.
femininity is not weakness.
femininity is not weakness.
femininity is not weakness.

- mantra #1

I wish I could erase every fairytale in my memory
that told me I needed to be saved
by someone other than myself

- accountability pt. 1

> I am too full
> to eat any more of
> your honey-dripped sentences.

- the heaviness in your voice keeps catching in my throat

you love so hard
you don't even notice
that
he's eating your heart for breakfast
and spitting out the leftovers for lunch

look down. you're running out.

everything inside you spells
run.
your eyes trace the shapes with each blink
your veins pump blood in cursive swirls
your tongue twitches around those three letters
run. run. run.

- it happened in November and the feeling never left
until I did

study the back of him.
watch him grow smaller with each step.
notice the softness in his pace.
do you still find him gentle?
can you still feel his tenderness in your palms?
when you replay this memory at 2 in the morning
will you find a breeze in your chest
or a rock in your stomach?

- when he leaves you

I cannot keep allowing myself
to get tangled in your warmth anymore.
the heat is building
and I don't remember the way out.

//winter

summer honey // winter rain

what do you do
when wolves take over your body
and you are nothing but jagged teeth and tail

I am fighting the urge to rip apart my insides
with each stride

I spend my nights howling at the moon for you

there is a shipwreck between my ribs and it took far too
        long for me to understand that this is what
                drowning feels like.

                            it's exhausting
                   carrying the ocean in my chest.

I come home and all I want is you.
it's like the air is different here or something.
it smells of us.
I drive past memories on my way to the grocery store.
I see your smile in my morning tea.
everything is coated in your presence.
everything smells like you
tastes like you
feels like you

home is where we were born.
I can't shake the desire to find the seed and
keep it growing.

I need to get out of here.

- stale

you gave me comfort.
you wrapped it in feathered blankets and handed it to me as
cautiously
and carefully
as your calloused hands could muster.
you stroked my cheeks with the back of your hand so
I wouldn't feel the roughness.
you wrapped me in your wilted arms each night
and didn't let go until the sun pried my eyes open.

you were every drop of tender I've never known.
I was suffocating in the warmth of it all.

- when everything is not enough

do not mistake warm bodies
and generous hands
for a home.

petals fall from my lips.
but I no longer want to speak to you with such softness.
you do not deserve my flowers.

I will grow them around my tongue
and press them into the palms of those who will
appreciate how delicate they are.

- (you do not need to bloom for everybody)

fill your bath with all the lukewarm love
you ever spat out.
dip your fingers in.
dip your toes in.
wash your freckles off.
wash your cracked lips.
hear the dullness of it splash the side of the tub.
watch it cling like you remember.

do not feel bad observing each drop
empty from beneath itself.
do not feel bad when it happens quickly.
do not feel bad to turn the faucet and start over.

- night rituals

you are going to love him more.

you are going to give and give
only to find empty hands and quiet rooms.
his indifference will fill you
and hollow you
and you will be left with saltwater
at your feet
and an ache in your stomach.

but you are going to love him.

each night you will taste his bitter tongue
and ask yourself
why you keep coming back for more
when
the well is dry
and you are dying of thirst.

my ocean is escaping beneath me
trying to drink in all the waves I gave you too quickly
filling my stomach back up with all the parts of myself
you let fall from open palms

- flood

sarah schwab

I am living in stolen bones.
It makes heaviness feel like home.

I just wish I could take my heart
and hold it outside of myself for a few moments

I need the chance to feel a
weightless
and
empty
ribcage

- s p a c e

scrub out the breath of his
I love yous
from your neck.
pull apart the syllables that once kept you awake
until the sun glazed over your bedroom window.
rub out any trace of yesterday from the corners of your
eyes.

- this is not a cleaning piece

don't you understand?
I have been trained to fear you
with your wide shoulders and grasping hands
the kind that
know more about taking than giving
that
tie me in knots and leave me to untangle myself.

I'm still not sure if I ever learned how.

I have lain beneath bodies with no willpower left to utter
the word they call magic,
as if one syllable will erase the beast that is too hungry to
hear anything besides his own breath -
forcing air into me and swallowing me whole.
as if magic is anywhere near me in this moment
as if a word could stop wolves from feeding.

let him devour his feast
because you don't have much of a choice
you are dinner
and he is hungry

with pursed lips and
turned backs
they showed me that questioning
anything
will drain the holiness from my body
they taught me that doubt and uncertainty
will turn me into stone
and remove all the softness I spent
years
sewing into myself

I became more afraid of
losing my faith
than losing myself

(it took giving it up to find her again)

- things they don't teach you in catholic school pt. 2

> we teach girls to be
> so small
> we lose track of them
> and at some point they become women
> but we never really stop treating them
> like we did before we lost them

- hey babygirl

pain must be felt to overcome. pain must be felt to overcome. pain must be felt to overcome. pain must be felt to overcome. pain must be felt to overcome. pain must be felt to overcome. pain must be felt to overcome. pain must be felt to overcome. pain must be felt to overcome. pain must be felt to overcome. pain must be felt to overcome. pain must be felt to overcome. pain must be felt to overcome. pain must be felt to overcome. pain must be felt to overcome. pain must be felt to overcome. pain must be felt to overcome. pain must be felt to overcome. pain must be felt to overcome. pain must be felt to overcome. pain must be felt to overcome. pain must be felt to overcome. pain must be felt to overcome. pain must be felt to overcome. pain must be felt to overcome. pain must be felt to overcome. pain must be felt to overcome. pain must be felt to overcome. pain must be felt to overcome. pain must be felt to overcome. pain must be felt to overcome. pain must be felt to overcome. pain must be felt to overcome. pain must be felt to overcome. pain must be felt to overcome.

- mantra #2

I just need a moment where my hands aren't
around my neck
so I can hold my heart
and feel the cracks

slowly
gently
alone

I ask you for a drink from the stream right behind you
you don't respond
and instead of getting the drink myself
I sit in my thirst and wonder
what I could do to get you to pour water into my mouth

- accountability pt. 2

my four year old self
lives in my ribcage.
she kicks and screams
and fights all the demons she never defeated.

But the demons are gone
and in their place are warm hands and safe homes.
I need to learn the difference
before they lock the doors.
before they run out of patience with the tantrum happening
in place of a heartbeat.

you may often feel like the world is crumbling
at your feet
the way your heart crawls up your throat
and your brain fills with rainwater.
but I promise
your heart will find its way home again.
the sky will pull all the water back into itself.
you will not feel like this forever.
try to get some rest.

- self-care sometimes means giving up on today knowing tomorrow might be better // anxiety attacks are not as forgiving as you are

I take parts of my soul
and I sprinkle them into the rivers before winter.
I hope you find a piece in spring.

// spring

summer honey // winter rain

you have to forgive yourself
every single day
every single hour
for all the pain your gentleness has caused you

look at me.
look at me.
my petals are opening
purple and orange
and yellow
like the women before me.
but you do not see how
I look in the sunlight.
how my
leaves curl
how my
stem is rooted.
you pulled me from my warmth
and pressed me between books
filled with all the words
I gave you
while you were sleeping.
I do not want them surrounding me.
I do not want to make a home of them.
I did not ask for you to give me water.
I just need you to move your hands
so I can catch the rain.

- thirsty

> Please.
> wring me dry

I forgot what the sun feels like on wanting skin.

I've always wondered what it'd be like
to never have birthed
art
from my womb.
To not have shared blood with a creature
so horrible
and
so lovely.
What it would be like
to not breathe up its flowered insides every morning
and spit them back out each night.
How empty my chest would feel
without the agony
and
wonder
of this gnawing thing.

-    birthing beasts

Take. Offense. To. Offensive. Things.

- (do not feel bad for feeling)

I sang my goodbyes through
gritted teeth.
pulled out every ache like a
stitch.
do not forget
what formed you
but do not be afraid
to watch the scar heal over
and
bury the memories along the way.

you will stumble over your own feet
trying to look steady for him
but you are the ocean.
let yourself rise and fall like you always have.
you do not need to empty yourself because you are
afraid
of your own waves.

                                I keep forgetting
                                           that
                                hungry stomachs
                           do not always ask for food
                    when they have a feast in front of them
                                  you are the feast
                               you are the nourishment
                              stop waiting for affirmation
                      when your whole body is filled with every
                                      delicious
                                         thing
                                    he could want

-    do not doubt it (you are everything)

I want to be open for you.
the way sunflowers chase sunlight
drinking in warmth with every petal.
the way rivers soften their way around
every obstacle.
I want to be a place for you to rest
a place to call home.

until then – between then – when my heart swallows the
room and leaves no space – when you can't find any more
air to fill me –

I will trace over every curve of my body that my heart still
lives in. I will become soaked in honey. I will learn to enjoy
the lightness of empty hands.
I will stop asking for pieces of you.

- accountability pt. 3

when they try to wrap you around each syllable
until you can fit in the palm of their hand,
remember
you were birthed in salt water,
you are made of mountains and valleys and
turn into stars at night.
you are the sound of the sun rising.
they cannot take away the breath of your spirit
without your permission.

- (don't give it to them)

how liberating
to be settled into my own bones
instead of yours.
to finally
sit in my skin without aching for you.
the air is so much cleaner here

alone.

my self-worth will not be reduced by anyone.
my self-worth will not be reduced by anyone.
my self-worth will not be reduced by anyone.
my self-worth will not be reduced by anyone.
my self-worth will not be reduced by anyone.
my self-worth will not be reduced by anyone.
my self-worth will not be reduced by anyone.
my self-worth will not be reduced by anyone.
my self-worth will not be reduced by anyone.
my self-worth will not be reduced by anyone.
my self-worth will not be reduced by anyone.
my self-worth will not be reduced by anyone.
my self-worth will not be reduced by anyone.
my self-worth will not be reduced by anyone.
my self-worth will not be reduced by anyone.
my self-worth will not be reduced by anyone.
my self-worth will not be reduced by anyone.

- mantra #3

Lessons in tenderheartedness
Be soft. Cry when you feel like it. Even if it's often
even if it's uncomfortable.
Take all the emotions swirling around you every
day and hold them over your heart and feel them
burrow their branches into your lungs and breathe
in deeper than you ever have before.
You are not weak just because you allow the world
to pool in your palms in the quiet moments.
You are powerful and strong and so, so brave.
Do you know that? Never let your open waters be
reduced by those that value walls over seas. Watch
the way the sky reflects itself onto your surface.
Observe the power of your own waves as they
crash into one another.
It's okay when you overflow.
You are the ocean.
Spill and refill.
Spill and refill.
Spill and refill.

your heart has been collecting all that winter salt
and all that summer sand
and it is heavy.

dip it in the river.
clear away the rot.
feel like fresh air again.

- spring cleaning

Feel the droplets hit your flesh.
Listen to them bounce off your rooftop.
Taste the chill of the flooded sky on your tongue.
Forget about all those times you mistook yourself for weak.
Forget about all those times you held back your storm for
the sake of someone else.
Forget about your bended knee and bitten tongue.
Forget everything that keeps you quiet.

It is impossible to fill yourself with everyone else without
spilling over.
Spill.
Pour.
Soak everything around you with your truth.
Do not mistake fluidity for placidity.
You were built for this.
Rain down.
Do not apologize.
Rain harder.

I need you to rain down sunlight on all the dark parts.
I need you to remind me that it's okay to grow slowly.

- how to tend a garden

I found you
on the cusp
of
finding myself

the full moon lives in my belly
and
light pours from my mouth
every time you ask for a sip.

keep drinking.

love is an accident.
it forms in between your
cracked fingers and
scarred knuckles
and doesn't show itself until you are
five feet deep in dirt
growing a garden you didn't know you wanted.
but as you look around at all of the bright blooms
and opening petals
you can't help but know this is exactly
where you are supposed to be.
and dirt under your fingernails feels good,
even if it rubs off on your new white blouse and
leaves streaks on the side of your face.
you feel prettier
somehow
with remnants of yesterday's growth marked onto
your flesh.

- blind

I have never felt more sure of anything.
I have never felt more terrified.

- soulmate

my relationship with you
is the closest reflection of myself I've ever seen.
we are ripping each other open and finding ourselves in there.
do you see how loudly my demons yell from your chest?

no one told me that loving you would teach me to heal all the parts of myself I thought I lost.

we found our homes
in the wrinkled corners of each other's souls.

they forget to tell you that growing hurts.
it breaks you and mends you with whatever you feed it.
feed it gold.
feed it fresh water and tenderness.
become stronger and brighter than anything you recognize.

you are sunlight.

throwing roses.
tearing paper.
painting everything bright yellow.
pretending to be the sun.

- healing

sarah schwab

//summer

summer honey // winter rain

the feeling of walking outside after it just rained.
                          at five in the morning.
when dirt covers your feet in pieces of yesterday.
            and you can feel the clouds in your lungs.

                        that's what my soul looks like.

I grew beneath lilac bushes and saw dust
above sprouting earth and sticky floors
with open windows
and dancing in the kitchen
and soup so hot it burned my tongue
but I didn't stop eating it
because every bite tasted exactly how home should feel
and every time it hit my lips I was reminded that
fire keeps souls alive
and this house will always be filled with over-boiling pots
because
we do not know how to love any other way

-    our loud and heavy love

there are many types of love stories.
cultivate all of them.

you wrapped your love in wrinkled newspaper
ink pulling itself off the pages
letter by letter
finding its way between each finger
writing a new story onto my palms.

you taught me that love can be simple
and silly
and imperfect.
that happy hearts give
without asking for anything in return
that love can be a state of being
and joy only multiples when shared.

you cracked open your chest.
sunlight
poured over everyone you met.
leaving them with streaks of yellow on
the backs of their hands
a burst of light
(pieces of you)
wherever they went.

- for the angels born as humans (I am so lucky to have known you)

watch the way your grandparents love
the way they ebb and flow
like they're dancing on the moon.
the way their hearts play the rhythm of your favorite song.
the song you could listen to forever.
the song that reminds you of belly laughs and tenderness.
of soft smiles and gentle hugs.
of giving. and giving. and giving.

can you feel it? that fullness in your chest?
their love fills every corner of the room.

(I take pieces every time I visit. I've collected a pile in my room and grab a handful whenever I need a reminder that I am a part of them.)

one night I swallowed a star
the next
an entire constellation

I kept eating pieces of the sky trying to find a light that would match yours.

now my belly is filled with beams of ancient dust
and
I hear your echo with every breath:

this light is yours now.
find every dark sky you can
and fill it with your galaxy.
I will meet you there
every time.

you bloom
because
your grandmother
and her grandmother
and hers
spent their lifetime
growing roots
and drinking sunlight.
they dreamed of the colors your petals would become
how your pollen would attract every bee and butterfly for
miles
how your leaves would curl around themselves into
tiny embraces.

in the first minutes of the morning
turn your ear towards the sun.
can you hear them? the humming in the breeze?
your ancestors are singing for you
are watching you bloom
are seeing your purples and yellows
and
offering you all the sunlight and rainwater they saved up
generation
after generation
they were waiting for you.

-    dandelion lion

Everything ends.
Good days. Bad days.
Difficult moments.
Vibrant memories.
Life itself.
If you are lucky, and you find yourself at the feet of
someone's final sunset
feel the brilliance and heartbreak
of that irreplaceable moment.
See how the whole space is filled with
soft yellows
and closing petals.
With waves lapping sandy shores
and
stardust peeking through wispy clouds.
Grab pieces of their warmth and then let them go
without fear.
Watch as they tuck themselves into the horizon
so gently and so quietly
you almost don't notice it's happening
until you are left with
stardust in your palms
and honey-soaked memories sewn into
every part of you.

You can be sad.
Let yourself become saltwater if you must.
Bust as you watch tomorrow's sun glisten on your
fingertips and the light warm your cheeks
know that each moment is filled with them.
Every time you step into that yellow light
your bones are filling with

every laugh
every embrace
every song they ever sung.
Like sunlight, ever-present and luminescent
they will be there.
In the hard times.
In the joyful moments.

They will warm you and leave you whole.

it comes to me in waves.
like secrets whispered over riverbanks.
I collect them one by one
until I have a novel in my lungs
full of soft hums and tenderness.
it sighs out of me in sentences
in pages
in chapters
until I am on my knees
your voice in my palms
your heartbeat smiling its way through me

- (did you know you'd become a part of me? I suppose you did.)

you are filled with
every
beautiful
word
I forgot the meaning to.

tell me them again.
it sounds like honey.
tell me them again.
you are honey.

- stories inside us

love is a state of being.
love is a state of being.
love is a state of being.
love is a state of being.
love is a state of being.
love is a state of being.
love is a state of being.
love is a state of being.
love is a state of being.
love is a state of being.
love is a state of being.
love is a state of being.
love is a state of being.
love is a state of being.
love is a state of being.
love is a state of being.
love is a state of being.
love is a state of being.
love is a state of being.
love is a state of being.

- mantra #4

you are the shade of yellow
my grandma talks about
when she's thinking of the sun
and her husband
and our favorite song.
you seep into my dreams and crackle my
eyelids with fireworks.
your every syllable feels like home.
a new home.
a home filled with bright red poppies and
smelling of sweet earth.
a home with stories taped to the walls
and empty coffee mugs by the bedside table.

- you have felt like fate since the first moment

there is so much beauty in the space between
light and
dark.
before they touch.
as they collide.
the softness of them together.

the hues of everything, right here.
between our fingertips.
between our torsos.
between our thighs.
how lucky are we
to see what the sky would look like
if it was every time all at once.

you pour salt water into my bones
        I am becoming the ocean.

it feels as sweet as
honey-soaked fingers.
it's like
the last breath of the setting sun,
deep
and bright
and radiating.
like a lovers hands through your hair,
down your spine.
like the crest of a wave as the tide goes down.

hold on
until your knuckles turn white.

- falling in

the month you forget.
the month it stops hurting
the month the heat kisses you
and leaves your skin wet.
the month you feel empty.
the month you meet a stranger that feels like home.

this is where you are.
this is where you wake up.
this is where you remember.

- August

I owe you
all the softness
you helped me find.
take handfuls from my cheeks.
watch them regrow.
watch them turn to the sun.
see how your fingerprints form swirls in my skin cells.
you are making me new again.
we are turning into something
I didn't know I could dream of.

- love like that

>   here we are
>   stripped down
>   honest and open and filled with the sky.
>   and I have never
>   *never*
>   felt more whole
>   more loved
>   more beautiful
>   than I do right now
>   at your side
>   in your easy embrace
>   soaked in your gaze
>   coated in your stardust

- you are everything my soul has ever craved

no other feeling
softens
and sets fire
in the same moment

- joy

I am blooming.
honey is spilling from my pores like it's
always belonged.
the sweet stickiness catching the sun's rays
and
shouting back at the sky
I am here!
I am alive!
I am happy!

can you feel it?
it's the softest heaviness I've ever had to carry.

your soul. your body.
is as strong as mountains.
you can take air from people's lungs
and give it back in the same breath.
you are filled with unmovable strength.
you are the boulder that shakes the earth.
the crown that kisses the clouds
you are filled with glorious
curves
and valleys
that hold whole entire ecosystems.
entire rainstorms.
never apologize for taking up space.
you were meant to be this grand
unforgettable
force of nature.

- earthling

look at yourself in the mirror
see how your hands fold over your hips
like papier-mâché
how your feet grip and release
like they are still learning how to carry you

study the arch of your knees
the dip in your spine
the peaks of your thighs
like steeples in a church
your body is a place of worship
you are holier than any god I've ever known.

- things they don't teach you in catholic school pt. 3

at first
you won't notice your growth.
it starts slow.
roots have to dig into the earth.
rainwater has to sing to you
day after day
until the most delicate parts of your palms
reach the sunlight.
until you become more open petals than darkness.
more intertwined branches than solitude.
admire all the ways you came to be here.
all that heartache.
all that love.
you have cracked open the earth and
spilled yourself onto it.
you deserve every second of this feeling.
wrap yourself in it.
be proud.
share it.
keep growing.

with honey in my throat
and
rain in my palms
pieces of myself
have collected onto each page
newness sewn into me.

I am not the same woman.
(I am exactly the same woman.)

Made in the USA
San Bernardino, CA
23 May 2018